canterbury

the story of a cathedral

Sally Rousham

Designed by Robin Wade Design
Associates/Michele Walker
Drawings by Geoffrey Bargery
Published by Carlton Cleeve Limited
for the Dean and Chapter
of Canterbury Cathedral

© Dean and Chapter of Christ Church, Canterbury, 1975
ISBN 0 90489 800 8
Printed in England by Ebenezer Baylis and Son Ltd, Leicester and London

foreword

Canterbury Cathedral has stood as a living witness to man's belief in God for more than nine hundred years. Its timeless beauty has been a source of spiritual inspiration to people all over the world. Day by day the worship of Almighty God is celebrated here and the Church's tradition of prayer and praise is maintained.

Each year millions of visitors come to Canterbury. The exhibition in the western Crypt is for their benefit. It is designed to increase their understanding of this great Cathedral, its building, its music, the people who have worked and do work in it, and the part it has played in British history.

At the time of the Canterbury Cathedral Appeal, it is particularly appropriate to focus attention on the significance of this, the Mother Church of English Christianity. It has stood for so much in the past and, God willing, will continue to do so for future generations.

July, 1975

IAN HUGH WHITE-THOMSON
Dean of Canterbury

acknowledgements

This booklet has been produced to complement the exhibition in the Crypt of Canterbury Cathedral which opened on 24th July, 1975. The exhibition was planned by a committee under the chairmanship of Canon A.M. Allchin. The members of the committee were: Miss A.M. Oakley (Cathedral Archivist and Librarian); Mr R.H. Brasier (Vesturer); Mr P.D. Marsh (Surveyor to the Fabric); Mr R.E. Steel (Manager, Cathedral Gifts Ltd); Miss S. Rousham; Mr R. Wade; Mr P. Saabor and Mr P.A. Taverner. Dr William Urry acted as academic adviser.

The Dean and Chapter wish to thank the many individuals, companies, and bodies who have helped to make the exhibition possible either by loaning objects or by giving their time and advice. They acknowledge in particular the help given by His Grace the Archbishop of Canterbury; the Trustees of the British Museum; the Curator of the City Museums, Canterbury; the Librarian, Lambeth Palace; Mr Douglas Hughes of the Whitechapel Bell Foundry; Mr Frederick Cole; Mr Brian LeMar; Dr Allan Wicks; Mr B.C. Doughty; Mr Colin Dudley; and Mr R.M. Dawson.

The exhibition was organised on behalf of the Dean and Chapter by Carlton Cleeve Limited and researched by Sally Rousham. It was designed by Robin Wade Design Associates/James Kingston-Stewart and Michele Walker. This booklet was written with the help of Anne Oakley.

contents

1 the cathedral boom

In Western Europe there was an extraordinary outburst of energy at the end of the eleventh century. Between 1050 and 1350 eighty cathedrals, five hundred large churches and thousands of parish churches were built. It has been estimated that by the end of the period there was one church for every two hundred people in many cities. Norwich had fifty churches, Lincoln only one less and York had forty-one. The height of Strasbourg cathedral was equal to a forty-storey skyscraper and a fourteen-storey building could have fitted *inside* the choir of Beauvais cathedral.

The Norman prelates who came to England after the conquest undertook the building of churches and cathedrals with astonishing zeal; Lanfranc set an example at Canterbury which was followed up and down the country. The architects of these buildings were Norman, but the craftsmen were Anglo-Saxons.

Men built cathedrals for a mixture of reasons. The construction of the building was itself an act of faith: men built for the glory of God. The fact that many of the decorations and most brilliant features of construction could not be seen by anyone standing in the building was irrelevant – God was all-seeing. The men working on the building felt that they were earning a place in heaven. There were also elements of motivation which became more common in later centuries. With the growth of cities and the development of a free and prosperous bourgeoisie personal aggrandisement and civic pride played their part.

The slowing down of the cathedral boom came towards the end of the thirteenth century. This was partly because men's faith was not so ebullient and a period of general stagnation had been reached. The outbreak of the Hundred Years War in France in 1337 inhibited building on the continent, and Europe entered one of its periodic financial crises.

LUND

COLOGNE
AACHEN
MAINZ
RHEIMS
WORMS
STRASBOURG
SPEYER
VEZELAY
FREIBURG
ULM
VIENNA
AUTUN

MILAN

VENICE

PISA
FLORENCE
SIENA
ORVIETO
ROME

PALERMO
MONREALE

3. Indenture to pray for Henry VII
and his family

Finance

To build Canterbury cathedral today would cost more than a hundred million pounds, and yet it was only one of thirty cathedrals be built in England and Wales during the Middle Ages. These tremendous building projects were financed in various ways.

The church received many gifts. People believed completely in the power of intercession whereby souls could be saved from hell by the prayers of righteous men. So they endowed chantry chapels or gave money towards the construction of churches. Often, as men got older or younger men fell sick, they made wills leaving their property or the income from their property to the church.

Christ Church Priory also received rents from the houses and shops that it owned in the precincts and the town, and from stalls set up for the fairs which were held in the precincts four times a year. It received manorial dues: the Priory owned property as far away as Norfolk and Devon. And it had the offerings made by pilgrims. The income fluctuated greatly, partly through variations in the number of pilgrims and partly because of weather and other farming conditions such as epidemics of cattle plague. Depending on the relative state of their finances, sometimes the monastery would borrow from the archbishop and sometimes vice versa. On other occasions they borrowed from the Jews or from Florentine bankers.

As an example of the financing of building works, one can take the reconstruction of the nave which was completed under Prior Chillenden (1391–1411). When it was discovered that the Norman nave was unsound, Archbishop Simon Sudbury invited subscriptions to the building fund and offered an indulgence of forty days to anyone who contributed. He also made a personal donation of three thousand marks. (A mark was equal to 13s 4d. and might represent as much as £80 in present-day purchasing power.) His successor, Archbishop Arundel, gave a thousand marks and the income from the rectories of Godmersham and Westwell. There were also royal donations: Richard II and Henry IV both contributed to the building work.

In the fifteenth century, as in the twentieth, building was financed partly by an annual grant from the corporate funds of the prior and convent and partly by outside help, including donations from the citizens of Canterbury. In 1831 when the Dean and Chapter decided to rebuild the north-west tower, they were empowered by a special Act of Parliament to raise a £20,000 mortgage on their properties to finance the project.

4. 12th century rental of Christ Church properties

5. Stages in the building of the Cathedral

2 the Building of christ church canterbury

There is no date to which one can point and say that was when Canterbury cathedral was built. The site of the present building was probably a centre of pagan worship long before the Christian era. The cathedral that stands today is not the realisation of a unified vision but is rather an accumulation of Christian architecture.

Augustine took over an old Roman Christian church when he established his mission in Canterbury; there would have been various attempts at rebuilding between then and the Norman invasion over four hundred years later. Reconstructions of the Saxon church are highly speculative, but it was certainly much smaller than the building that replaced it. In 1066 Canterbury submitted quickly to the Normans and as a result was spared much destruction. However, the Saxon church was accidentally burnt down in 1067; though the Normans were compulsive builders and would have pulled it down sooner or later.

Lanfranc was already seventy when William the Conqueror brought him from Bec to be Archbishop of Canterbury, but he was a man of remarkable optimism and energy and played a vital part in the building of the new cathedral. It was completed in the incredible time of seven years.

By the time Anselm was archbishop, the cathedral was considered to be too small and was also showing signs of foundering. While Anselm was primate Ernulf was prior and he was the genius who designed the western crypt that stands today. It was not possible to obtain the land to follow the usual practice of lengthening the nave so the church was extended eastwards by the construction of a remarkably long choir. Unfortunately this part of the building was destroyed by a disastrous fire in 1174.

6. The crypt built by Prior Ernulf

7. The choir built by William of Sens

8. The nave built by Henry Yevele

The new choir that replaced the one built by Ernulf and his successor, Prior Conrad, had to accommodate the hordes of pilgrims who came to do homage at the shrine of Thomas Becket. William of Sens was the architect of this work, but after he had been badly injured by a fall from the scaffolding his job was finished by another William, the Englishman. This second William built the eastern crypt and the Trinity Chapel and corona above.

By the end of the fourteenth century a new nave had to be constructed and the man employed to do this was Henry Yevele, the architect of Westminster Abbey and the Charterhouse in London as well as other famous buildings. It is his nave and transepts that stand today.

The last significant addition to the cathedral was the construction of the famous central tower – the Angel Steeple or Bell Harry Tower as it is called – by John

Wastell during the priorate of William Sellinge. This was completed in 1499 and is a magnificent example of 'decorated' architecture at its most successful. The upper part of this tower is constructed of 480,000 'redde bryks' which were used for the inside work while the ashlar coating was done with stone from Caen in Normandy and Merstham in Surrey.

The cathedral had yet to face first the Reformation and then the civil war and the period of Puritan domination. At the instigation of Henry VIII all shrines were removed together with any images of Becket, but greater destruction came during the Civil War in the seventeenth century. The iconoclasts went to great lengths to destroy all statues and other images and they broke much of the stained glass. For years no services were held in the cathedral: a sermon was preached in the chapter house every Sunday and Bell Harry rang only once a week to announce the opening of the town market.

When Charles II was restored to the throne in May 1660, he landed at Dover and spent his first night in Canterbury. He went to a service in the cathedral the next day but was dismayed by the dilapidation and neglect. The Dean described the church as being in a 'sad, forlorn, and languishing condition'. In the years which followed much was done to refurbish the cathedral, particularly in the choir which was fitted out with splendid woodwork.

The next hazard that confronted the fabric of the building was the nineteenth century. At Canterbury the Victorians did their best to honour the cathedral, but their activities were sometimes unfortunate. During the Gothic revival it was thought that everything in a Gothic building should be of the period. An architect surveyed Lanfranc's surviving north-west tower and advised that it would be possible and desirable to restore it; however his advice was ignored and the Dean and Chapter opted for rebuilding.

During the Second World War the cathedral was threatened with destruction. Enemy bombing flattened much of the town and precincts, but miraculously the church survived. Since then polluted air has done much to dilapidate the fabric. A programme of refurbishing is under way, but this is restoration, not development.

3 the Builders

The master-mason was the most important man in the building of a cathedral; it was he who developed into what we would call a professional architect. The first master-mason whom we really know about is William of Sens, the architect who built the choir of Canterbury. Gervase, the twelfth century chronicler, tells us how, after the fire of 1174, the monks 'consulted how, and by what method, the ruined church might be repaired. Architects, both French and English, were therefore assembled; but they disagreed in their opinions; some undertook to repair, while others, on the contrary, affirmed that the whole church must be taken down if the monks wished to dwell in safety . . . Among the architects there was one, William of Sens, a man of great abilities, and a most curious workman in wood and stone. Neglecting the rest, him they chose for the undertaking. And to him and to providence was the work of God committed.' It was William of Sens who gave the choir its strikingly French appearance.

The mason often started his career in the quarry and worked through the various grades – hewer, rough mason, free mason, carver. Many masons spent three or four years travelling around Europe after they had completed their training, working first at one site and then another. This helps to account for the rapid spread of architectural styles. In the Romanesque and early Gothic periods of building the mason was a craftsman as well as a designer, but by the end of the thirteenth century he was becoming more and more a source of instruction and less an active craftsman.

Master-masons were literate and could usually speak some Latin and French. Gothic architecture would not have been possible without an understanding of geometry and the rules of proportion; a

11

knowledge of classical geometry came down to Western Europe via the Arabs. The status of the architect master-mason was that of an esquire at court and he was usually able to live a comparatively comfortable and prosperous life.

On every major building site a thatched hut was constructed where the masons were able to eat and rest and where they could work on the shaping of stone. This hut, which might have sheltered about twenty masons, came to be known as the lodge (it is from this that we get the freemasons' lodge of today). Gradually a type of guild organisation grew up and by the fifteenth century we find masons becoming an exclusive body and, like other guilds, keeping trade secrets.

The architects sometimes drew their plans on parchment, but it seems that more often the plan of the cathedral was incised on a plaster slab (examples have survived at Wells and York). It must have been necessary to modify these plans over the years as the building progressed. To get the shape of the columns and arches the architects made profiles of the mouldings which were cut out and used as templates by the masons. Zinc templates are used in the mason's yard in the same way today.

Most of the stone used for building the cathedral at Canterbury came from Caen in Normandy; it was easier to transport it across the Channel to Fordwich than to haul it overland from an English quarry. In his biography of Lanfranc, Milo Crispinus says 'he caused to be brought over the sea in swift-sailing vessels squared stones from Caen, in order to build with'. The stone was cut and dressed in the quarry to make it lighter and easier to transport. It was marked first with the personal sign of the workman who cut it and secondly with a number indicating the exact position where it was to go in the building.

Caen stone was used right into the nineteenth century but it deteriorates in modern atmospheric conditions and nowadays Lepine stone is used for work on the cathedral.

Purbeck stone from Dorset was first used in England by William of Sens at Canterbury. It was a fashion that came from Flanders and it led to the evolution of a class of masons called marblers.

There was an army of unskilled labour at work on the building as well as the masons and other craftsmen. These men (and even women occasionally) were usually recruited locally. They did the digging and levelling, they carried stone and mortar and worked the pulleys and winches. Some clever and diligent labourers were able to become craftsmen. There was always a shortage of skilled labour and the king had the power to impress both craftsmen and labourers to work on his building projects; this right was sometimes extended to ecclesiastical builders.

The stages of building

Canterbury was typical of medieval cathedral building in that the cathedral was not started from scratch but always replaced an earlier building. Usually the first job to be done was demolition and the clearing of the site. When this had been completed the central axis of the new building could be pegged out and then right angles taken from that line (using the 3:4:5 triangle); all other measurements would follow from these. If new foundations had to be laid, trenches were dug and filled with rubble and then lime mortar. The first course of dressed stone was set on this.

While this work was being done the master-mason and master-carpenter would be away selecting the stone and wood to be used.

The building season, even in the south-east of England, lasted only from March to October and then all the unfinished work had to be thatched to protect it from frost. During the winter a large part of the workforce was laid off and the men who had farms and families were able to go home. Provided the funds were available to pay them, skilled masons

10. Stonemasons' marks

13

11. Wooden centering

were kept on to cut and carve stone while carpenters would be preparing centering and other equipment for the next building season.

The skill of the early Norman builders did not always match their aspirations and some of their buildings did collapse – usually due to unstable foundations or poor craftsmanship. As we have seen, Lanfranc's cathedral became unstable after it had been standing for only seven years. Many Romanesque arches can be seen to be askew; this is because the mortar took months to set hard and the centering was taken away too soon. However, in the Gothic period centering was very skillfully and accurately constructed.

The years between 1050 and 1250 were a time of development, but between the later thirteenth century and the sixteenth century building techniques did not change dramatically. (Appearances altered, however, as walls became thinner and windows got much larger.) In early years the stone figures that decorate the cathedrals were sculpted *in situ* with an axe, as were the capitals in Ernulf's crypt, but from the thirteenth century most of the carving was done with chisels in the mason's lodge. At the beginning of the twelfth century the masons were still building with rather rough stones but they soon changed to using finely worked ashlar which was set closer together, this made construction much more precise. Building styles were influenced by the observations of the crusaders and the prisoners they brought back to Europe, some of whom were skilled craftsmen.

The Woodworkers

Meanwhile the carpenters had been at work. They had to build the workman's huts before any construction began. They designed and constructed centering and scaffolding and, of course, they made the roof. Even in the twelfth century good timber was hard to find and looking for suitable trees was an important part of the carpenter's work. Most of the wood used in the construction of Canterbury cathedral came from Blean Hill just outside the city (this land was owned by the church until recent times).

The massive roof trusses were cut out and assembled on the ground and then taken apart and hoisted into position and reassembled. Wooden pins and mortice and tenon joints were used for the junctions.

When the roof timbers were in place the plumbers covered them with cast sheet lead. These men worked with great skill – many Norman lead roofs survive to this day as witness. When the roof was covered the vault below could be constructed.

12. Treadwheel in Bell Harry Tower

13. Beams in the Cathedral roof

14. The roof over the north-west transept

15

In the Norman and early Gothic buildings there was not the mass of joinery work that later filled churches and cathedrals. In Canterbury the first wooden seating would have been the choirstalls which were built to rest the monks during their long hours of standing. On the underside of these tip-up seats were ledges called misericords which the elderly monk could lean upon to take some of the weight off his legs while apparently remaining standing.

In early churches the congregation stood through the service, though often there were stone benches running along the walls which the old or infirm could sit on. Wooden benches began to be used in the naves of parish churches in the thirteenth century, but permanent seating was not usually installed in the cathedrals. Benches and then more comfortable pews became necessary with the long sermons that were preached in later years.

The woodcarvers often decorated the church furniture: pulpits, font covers, screens, bench ends, choir stalls and misericords were often beautifully carved. Not many wooden monuments survive in churches today but there is a fine wooden effigy of Archbishop Peckham (d.1294) in the north transept of Canterbury cathedral.

The Smithy

The carpenters could not construct the first shed nor the masons hew the first stone without proper implements. It was the blacksmith who made the tools which were essential from the start of operations. The smith made and sharpened all the tools, made clamps, hooks and nails and the chains that were embedded in the walls for reinforcement. He also shod the horses on the site. The storage chests made by the joiner would have had hinges, bands and locks made by the smith (in later years the craft of the locksmith became a separate trade). The smith also produced hinges for the doors and grilles to protect tombs and reliquaries.

There would have been more than one forge on a cathedral construction site and at least another one in the quarry. Some smiths went from one site to another and there was a recognised class of itinerant bellows repairers. The smith had two or three assistants, a 'servant of the bellows and striker' and a lad to go round collecting the tools for sharpening.

STAINED GLASS

Canterbury cathedral has some of the most magnificent stained glass in England. As well as having a superb decorative effect, the glass was there to teach. At a time when few people could read, the pictures

15. The making of stained glass

seen in the church were a key method of instructing people in the faith.

Glass was made by heating sand, lime and potash in a furnace until they were white hot at which point they fused into liquid glass. When partially cooled the soft glass was picked up on a pipe and blown into a cylinder which was then cut open, flattened and left to harden.

Coloured glass was produced by adding various metal oxides to the original mixture. Iron oxide made yellows and greens, cobalt made blue, manganese made purple, and copper made the colour called 'ruby'. Because of the density of the ruby and the cost of the oxide, the colour was often 'flashed' onto the surface of a lighter glass which made it more transparent. The impurities in the molten glass and the variable thickness added the richness to early windows which was lacking in the thinner, clearer and smoother glass of later years.

Details of the glass pictures such as features and the folds of drapery were painted onto the glass and then fused on by firing.

The design of a stained glass window was drawn onto the white-washed top of a trestle table. The lines of the leads were then painted on; this was called a cartoon. The glass was then cut to shape by using a hot iron and cold water and then trimmed with a grozing iron. (Glass cutters were not used before the seventeenth century.) At this stage details were painted on and the glass was fired in the kilns. The pieces of glass were held together with strips of lead which had grooves in either side for the glass. The joints in the lead were soldered together on both sides. The stained glass was then installed in the cathedral. To prevent a large area of glass being blown in it was supported by an iron framework made by the blacksmith.

The techniques described here have changed little in practice and not at all in principle; they are as valid today as when Lanfranc came

19th century engravings of bell founding
16. Finishing the cope

17. Placing the cope over the core

18. Tuning the bell

to Canterbury.

The glass in the cathedral did not suffer when Henry VIII ordered the destruction of all images of Becket, but trouble was to come from the Puritans in the following century. In 1642 Richard Culmer, the infamous iconoclast, boasted in a letter 'When the [parliamentary] Commissioners entered upon the execution of that Ordinance in that Cathedral, they knew not where to begin, the images and pictures were so numerous, as if that superstitious Cathedral had been built for no other end but to stable idolls . . . A minister [Culmer himself] being then at the top of the citie ladder nearly 60 steps high, with a whole pike in his hand rattling down proud Becket's glassy bones . . .'

THE BELLS

In the days when there were no clocks there had to be some means of calling the faithful to church. The early Christians were a persecuted minority and could only use a handbell to announce the start of a service. But from the fifth century there was no need for secrecy and in the next few hundred years there are more and more references to church bells, though very few examples have survived.

The medieval craftsman made a model of the bell with a solid core. This was covered with wax to the shape of the finished bell

18

and on top of that was the 'cope' or outer mould. The models were made of a sandy clay mixed with cow dung and horse hair. The mould was then baked and the wax melted out. The hardened mould was then dug into a pit to give it the strength to withstand the pressure of molten bronze which was poured into it. Bell metal is three parts copper to one part tin (it is a myth that silver in the alloy improves the tone – the reverse is true). The principles of bell-founding have not changed.

Sometimes bells were cast on location and sometimes they were made in the foundry and transported, usually by water, to the church. In early days clerics made their own bells – St Dunstan was a skilled bell-founder – but during the Middle Ages it became a lay occupation and foundries were established in many cities.

Early bells were more cylindrical than the modern 'bell bottom' shape which was adopted during the thirteenth century and produced a much better tone. Wooden templates were used to get the shape of the core and the cope more uniform; this became much more important in the seventeenth century with the introduction of change ringing when bells had to be in tune with one another.

A bell is tuned by lessening the thickness of the rim or sound bow; pieces of the metal were chipped off the rim to lower the tone (it could not, of course, be altered upwards).

In 1668 Fabian Stedman published his *Campanalogia* which established the practice of change ringing in England. This fashion for ringing bells in a mathematical sequence rather than in tunes did not spread to the continent where 'carillons' are still rung. There is a 'ring' of twelve bells at Canterbury and it would take thirty-eight years to ring all the changes.

Bells are always referred to as 'she' – even Great Dunstan and Bell Harry at Canterbury. They were often named after saints or their donors. Bell Harry was named after Prior Henry of Eastry.

Not all bells were inscribed or even dated and often they merely carry the name of the donor or manufacture. Before the Reformation most of the longer inscriptions were religious, but some charming later examples have come down to us. A common seventeenth century inscription was 'I to the church the living call and to the grave do summon all'. One in Devon proclaimed 'true hearts and sound bottoms' – a reference to the wooden ships built in the area; in Bath Abbey: 'all ye of Bath who hear me sound, thank Lady Hopton's hundred pound'; and a simple boast in Bradfield, Essex: 'I am koc of this floc'.

19. Fifteenth century plainsong

4 cathedral music

'Touching musical harmony . . . such is the force thereof, and so pleasing effects it hath in that very part of man which is most divine, that some have been thereby induced to think that the soul itself by nature is or hath in it harmony.' So wrote Richard Hooker at the end of the sixteenth century in his defence of English church music against the attacks of the Puritans. Nonetheless, music has held a slightly ambiguous place in church life because of its dual nature – it can intensify religious experience or it can be a source of sensuous pleasure. But from the earliest times it has played a part in Christian worship, as it had done in the Jewish synagogue for centuries before. The liturgy was chanted in unison; this 'plainsong' began to be codified under Pope Gregory the Great and Gregorian chant is still the official liturgical music of the Roman Catholic church.

St Augustine of Canterbury brought music to England, although a standard system of notation had not been devised at that time. The chanting of plainsong was always of a high standard in England, second only to Rome. In the Priory the liturgy was chanted by the monks, but in the late Middle Ages on Sundays and feast days they were supplemented by paid singers from outside the community.

If boys were going to sing with men they had to sing an octave higher and from this the practice of harmony gradually developed. In the ninth and tenth centuries people began to sing the melody in two parallel parts – one a fifth or a fourth below the other. Looking back from this distance in time it is easy to see how this developed into polyphony – when two or more different but complementary melodies were sung together.

We know more about early sacred music than we do about secular music because it was the monks who developed a system for writing down music and because they are the source of most of our information. But music is infectious and the troubadours and the monks must have been influenced by each other's work. The secular melody that is still popular today, 'Summer is icumen in', was composed by a monk in the thirteenth century.

Canterbury has a strong musical tradition; the choir school there was the oldest in the country; there was a boys' choir from the mid-fourteenth century. Paid choristers became part of the cathedral establishment with the new foundation in the reign of Henry VIII 'that the praises of God may every day be celebrated with singing and thanksgiving'. The quality of music depended so much on the choir boys that in the sixteenth century there was hot competition for good singers. In the cathedral archives there is a reference to a boy being kidnapped from Canterbury to sing in the Chapel Royal.

A cathedral was often the centre of musical life in a community as it is today. John Merbecke was associated with the cathedral and Thomas Tallis sang in the choir. Orlando Gibbons died in Canterbury and is commemorated in the cathedral. Tallis and Merbecke lived through the Reformation during which time simpler music was introduced into the Church and the congregation joined in the singing which was, for the first time, in English. The first musical setting of the Anglican service was the 'Booke of Common Praier Noted' by Merbecke.

The Puritans had a stern attitude to music: they objected to organs in church and many were destroyed including the one in the cathedral which was 'spoiled' in 1642. Singing was made very simple indeed, with one note to each syllable; the choir at Canterbury was disbanded.

With the restoration of the monarchy in 1660, the tradition of church music was taken up again, and some outstanding composers wrote for the church in the later part of the century, chief among them Henry Purcell.

A great increase in congregational participation in church music came with the singing of hymns. Hymn singing developed outside the Church of England. Luther appreciated the importance of singing; 'why should the devil have all the best tunes?': a simple text and easy melody was a good way of teaching Christian doctrine – a view shared by John and Charles Wesley in the eighteenth century and by General Booth and the Salvation Army many years later. Hymns were being sung in churches by the end of the eighteenth century but it was not until later that they became a definite part of worship in the Church of England.

In the nineteenth century church music generally was at a low ebb.

20. An organ from the Canterbury Psalter

Choirs were poorly paid even by the standards of the time and the choir schools were in a dreadful state. In our own century, however, standards of cathedral music have greatly improved.

In parish churches before the nineteenth century the music was often provided by the village orchestra, but this did not happen in the cathedrals. After the Reformation sackbuts and cornetts accompanied the choir of Christ Church to support the boy singers, but the organ was the only instrument constantly played in the cathedral.

The Organ

Canterbury was one of the first churches in the country to have an organ. Archbishop Theodore is believed to have brought the first one to England in the seventh century. We know that St Dunstan set up organs in the abbey churches at Malmesbury and Abingdon.

The organ is descended from pan pipes. The size of organs has varied from the small 'portative' organ made in the Middle Ages to the giant organs of the nineteenth century. Since the sixteenth century the big organs have had a pedal keyboard and as many as five manual keyboards. A constant supply of wind is needed to play the organ. The earliest instruments had bellows like those used by the blacksmith and must have been very tiring to operate. Muscle power worked the bellows until the nineteenth century when steam was used, and in the twentieth century electric blowers have been developed to provide the wind.

23

21. Prior Sellinge, Henry VII and
Cardinal Morton from a 14th
century woodcarving

5 the monastery

All monastic institutions in Western Europe can be traced back to Benedict of Nursia (c.480–c.547). At various times in succeeding centuries new orders of monks and friars were established in England. These orders varied their emphasis. For example, the Cluniacs devoted themselves almost entirely to liturgical worship, the Cistercians lived a life of silence and manual labour and were great agricultural workers, and the friars were mendicants devoted to teaching and preaching, but they all owed their original inspiration to St Benedict. Benedict himself looked back to St Antony and the first Christian monks in Egypt and Palestine – the 'Desert Fathers'.

There were monks in Canterbury from the time of St Augustine, but Christ Church Priory was not 'regularised' until the reforms carried out by Archbishop Lanfranc after the Norman Conquest.

The head of an ordinary monastery was the abbot; in a cathedral monastery like Christ Church the bishop was the titular abbot but the man really in charge of affairs was the prior. Originally the archbishop appointed the prior, but from the end of the twelfth century he was elected by the brethren and there was often conflict and rivalry between prior and primate. Especially after the murder of Becket, the priors of Christ Church were men of some consequence, living in their own residence, often in great style, at one time it was even asserted that they had the right to choose the archbishop.

The centre of monastic life was the church and the 'Opus Dei' – the work of God – the divine service and the perpetual offering of prayer to God. Nine times a day the monks went into the church for services, one of which was a solemn celebration of the mass.

Like other monastic houses, the quality of life in the priory varied and from time to time there were movements of reform. Canterbury was a large and prosperous establishment; being in the middle of the city the monks inevitably found themselves much involved in worldly affairs. There were many other Benedictine houses in remoter parts of England that were very small and poor.

At one time monks used to join the community as children, but this practice died out during the twelfth century and novices were thereafter usually young men of about eighteen. Monks tended to come from more prosperous families and they often brought considerable wealth with them, but once they were members of the order all property was communally owned and social position counted for little or nothing. By the end of the twelfth century the monks owned nearly half of all the domestic property in Canterbury as well as their holdings outside the town. The income from the various properties was allocated to specific departments of the monastery, for instance the cellarer or the sacrist.

Library and Scriptorium

Benedictine monks were expected to spend some time in reading and study. Lanfranc's *Constitutions* set out that one day a year ' . . . the librarian shall have a carpet laid down, and all books got together upon it, except those which a year previously had been assigned for reading. These the brethren are to bring with them when they come to the chapter house, each his book in his hand . . . he whose conscience accuses him of not having read the book . . . is to fall on his face, confess his fault and entreat forgiveness . . . ' after which the librarian made a fresh distribution of books.

In the early days of the monastery there was not a library as such but a collection of books kept in cupboards and chests. The first complete catalogue of books was compiled during the priorate of Henry of Eastry (1284–1331) and lists 1,831 volumes – on theology and canon law and also the classics, science and history.

The writing and copying of books took place in the scriptorium which was probably located in the cloister, but we do not know exactly where. A distinctive and beautiful style of writing known as the Canterbury script was developed in the eleventh and twelfth centuries. Writing was done on parchment with goose quill pens; brushes were made by setting the tail hairs of ermine in quills. Colour pigments for the illuminations were made from small quantities of earths and minerals ground to powder and mixed with white of egg.

Religious houses were expected to provide hospitality. Before 1174 pilgrims to Canterbury were not numerous, and most travellers who

22. The monk Eadwine from the Canterbury Psalter

Incipit passio Sci ypoliti martiris
sociorumque eius. iii Augusti

E
GRES
SUS
BEA
TUS
ypo
LITUS

post tertium diem passionis sci
LAVRENTII venit indomum suam.

23. Initial from the *Legenda Sanctorum*, c.1125

24. The Saxon sundial

25. Hubert Walter's vestments/chalice   paten

mitre   orphrey   buskins

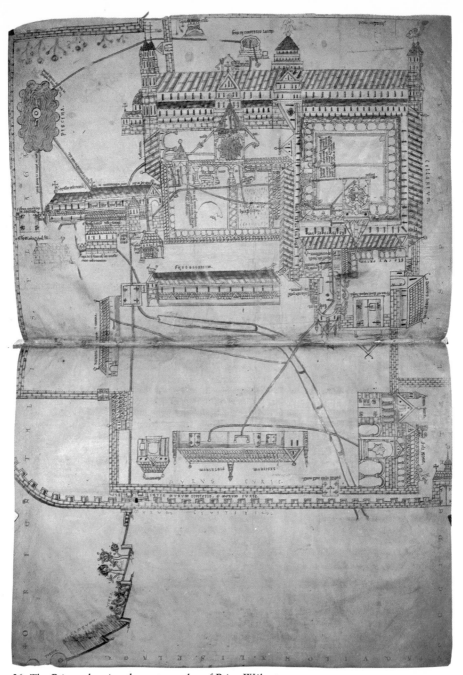

26. The Priory showing the waterworks of Prior Wibert

stayed there were on church or state business: Canterbury was on the route from London to the continent. The monasteries had special guest houses where visitors were welcomed for one or two nights (permission was required for a longer stay). The guest usually made gifts to the community but prolonged visits, especially by royalty, were a serious drain on resources. As it became a great centre of pilgrimage after the murder of Becket, Canterbury developed elaborate arrangements for coping with the huge numbers of visitors.

Another social function of the monasteries was the distribution of alms. At a time when there were no social services, not even a Poor Law, the charity of a religious house was the only hope of a destitute man or woman faced with starvation.

By medieval standards monasteries were clean places, especially Christ Church. The highly sophisticated waterworks system installed at Canterbury by Prior Wibert accounted for the fact that the monks suffered less than most people from the ravages of the Black Death. Baths were compulsory at Christmas and optional at other times of the year. Underwear was washed every three weeks in winter and every two in summer. Tonsures were shaved every three weeks.

At its peak, the Priory at Canterbury probably consisted of about one hundred and fifty monks plus almost as many servants. At this time there were about a thousand monastic houses of one order or another all over England with an estimated 17,000 inhabitants. After the Black Death of 1348–9 numbers declined and at the time of the dissolution of the monasteries there were about ten thousand monks. Christ Church seems to have had only a couple of dozen inmates when it was dissolved in 1540.

The break with Rome and the papacy had been made in 1534 and all but a few of the clerics in England had taken the oath of allegiance to the crown; however, Henry VIII decided to dissolve every religious community in England and sequester the property that had belonged to the great houses. The monks were absolved from their oaths and pensioned off to lead secular lives. While there was laxity at the beginning of the sixteenth century and some establishments were far too rich for their own good, greatly exaggerated tales of monastic corruption were put about to soften public opinion.

The priory at Canterbury was gone and the church was re-established as a 'secular cathedral' – a college of canons governed by a Dean and Chapter. The first Dean was the amazing Nicholas Wotton who weathered all the religious and political storms of the mid-sixteenth century and held his posts through the troublesome reigns of Henry VIII, Edward VI, Mary and Elizabeth I.

27. Coin of King Cnut

28. Penny of King John

29. Half-groat of Edward IV

32

6 coins and seals

Coinage is an indication of the sophistication and strength of an economy: it becomes necessary when life is too complex for barter to satisfy the needs of society. A coin with the head of a man stamped on it was both a symbol and a demonstration of that man's power.

Canterbury is important in the history of English coinage. The local mints served the kings of Kent and also produced coins for Offa, the most powerful king in England during the eighth century. It was during the reign of Offa that the silver penny replaced the old sceatta and the first penny was struck in Canterbury. For centuries the penny was the only coin minted; for smaller units it was cut into halves or quarters.

Before the minting of coins was centralised early in the thirteenth century, Canterbury had seven 'moneyers' (at a time when London had eight). During the reign of Henry II Canterbury was the most prolific mint in the country and there was a mint in the town until the middle of the sixteenth century. Until some time in the fourteenth or fifteenth centuries the archbishops had the privilege of minting coins themselves, though in the later years they were sometimes merely given a share of the profits from the mint.

Seals, unlike coins, had little intrinsic value but were symbolic. They had three functions: 1. they authenticated documents, supplementing or taking the place of a signature at a time when few people could write; 2. they secured documents or letters – in fact they sealed them; and 3. they were a means of identifying a person, for example a messenger.

The Pope used a seal of which impressions were made in lead, the celebrated papal *bulla*, which gave a name to the document which it authenticated. The archives of Canterbury cathedral contain several papal bulls, one or two still bearing the leaden *bulla*.

Seals have been used since biblical times. By the tenth century most bishops had their own seals and the custom spread not only through the church and the nobility but guilds, farmers and merchants had their own seals by the fourteenth century.

Medieval seals were varied in shape, but were most commonly large rounds for state seals, pointed ovals for noble women and for clerics, and smaller rounds with heraldic devices for noble families.

From the sixteenth century onwards, with the spread of literacy, the seal as a means of authentication became a mere formality for official documents as it still is today.

30. Seal press used by the Priory

31. Document with seals of bishops and Prior Henry of Eastry

34. Priory seal showing the martyrdom of Becket

32. The first known seal of the Priory

35. Matrices for seal of Dean and Chapter, 1770

33. Seal of Henry VIII

36. Seal of Eleanor of Castile

37. The Priest   38. The Wife of Bath

39. Chaucer
Pilgrims from the Ellesmere edition of Chaucer

7 pilgrimage

Two million people visit Canterbury every year and many of these are making a pilgrimage. Most religions have had places which were believed to be especially holy. Christian pilgrimage started in the third and fourth centuries and has continued to the present day; it reached its zenith in the later Middle Ages.

Men and women went on pilgrimages for widely differing reasons, often their motives were consciously or unconsciously mixed. For some it was an expression of sincere faith or a general religious exercise to achieve a state of grace; others undertook a pilgrimage as an act of penance or to honour a vow made at a moment of stress. Some people just had the urge to travel. Occasionally pilgrimages were undertaken on another's behalf; Archbishop Chichele, for example, requested in his will that a suitable chaplain should go on a pilgrimage for him. For many people pilgrimage was an escape from the close confines of their feudal lives, the nearest they would ever get to a holiday in the modern sense.

All sorts of people went on pilgrimages: kings, noble men and women, bishops, monks, nuns, and common folk of all ages were to be seen. Some travelled alone, others in groups. A few travelled on well-bred horses, more on asses, and many on foot. The word 'canter' came into the language from the easy gallop at which pilgrims rode to Canterbury. Most pilgrims paid their way, though some went begging. It was considered right to help and protect a pilgrim and in return people were usually glad to hear news from a stranger. The national boundaries that have since divided Europe scarcely existed then – all countries were part of Christendom.

A pilgrimage could be local – to the nearest shrine where the relics of some saint were kept, or it could involve hundreds of miles of travel to Rome or even as far as Jerusalem. It took about seven weeks to go from London to Saint Denis and back, eighteen to Rome or Compostela, and a year to go to Jerusalem.

Travel was not easy, especially if it involved going overseas. The worst hazard was the weather and there was always the risk of catching the plague or some other endemic disease. Kings and popes made some provision for protecting pilgrims but any journey could be brought to a sudden end by thieves or murderers. A pilgrim would have made his will before leaving home and he usually obtained 'testimonials' from his bishop and had his staff and scrip blessed.

It is difficult for us today to appreciate the veneration people had for relics. Any fragment of a saint's body or other object with holy associations was revered. The most solemn oaths were sworn not on the gospel but on relics. Educated people realised that many of the arms of saints, pieces of the True Cross or thorns from Christ's crown must have been false, but this did not lessen the goodness of the motive. A shrine acted as a focus of belief, it was where people could feel God's power. The relic of a saint acted as an intercessor.

At the shrines indulgences were offered to pilgrims as a form of reward. An indulgence did not constitute forgiveness for a sin but it did let the person off having to do the penance that was imposed when absolution was granted. It is probable that then, as now, people misunderstood the function of indulgences and thought they had been given licence to behave as they pleased. Anyone who has read Chaucer's *Canterbury Tales* will know that the sale of indulgences came to be abused.

Monasteries were sometimes founded on the site of a shrine, and their prosperity frequently depended on the popularity of that shrine as a centre of pilgrimage. Pilgrims usually made gifts of money or jewellery and some places, like Canterbury, accumulated tremendous riches. There was great competition for relics: some were sold by one religious house to another and sometimes what we would regard as shameless deception was used to obtain valuable relics.

Canterbury was a minor centre of pilgrimage long before the martyrdom of Thomas Becket. As well as the bodies of saints Alphege, Anselm, and Dunstan, Christ Church had the heads of three other saints, and the arms of eleven more, fragments of the True Cross, a thorn from Christ's crown, Aaron's rod, wool woven by the Virgin Mary and some of the clay out of which God had made Adam. However, it was after the death of Becket that the city attracted pilgrims from all over Europe. Until 1170 it had been a comparatively small town but almost overnight it became one of the holy places of

Christendom and it grew and prospered.

The most famous of all pilgrimages to Canterbury was that made by Henry II as penance for the murder of his archbishop: he walked barefoot through the town and was given five strokes with a rod from each bishop and abbot and three from each of the eighty monks. It was taken as a sign of forgiveness that within a week of the act the threats to Henry's kingdom from both Scotland and Flanders had receded.

Louis VII of France visited the shrine in 1179 and presented to it the fabulous 'French Regale' jewel and he also granted the convent a hundred 'muys' of wine a year in perpetuity. Other famous pilgrims included Richard I, King John, William the Lion of Scotland, and Henry VI.

There was a flood of pilgrims to Canterbury early in the thirteenth century and then on the jubilees of Becket's death in 1270 and 1320, but by the middle of the fifteenth century enthusiasm was fading. Erasmus was a sceptical visitor to the cathedral in 1512, but he was impressed by some things: 'The church dedicated to St Thomas, erects itself to Heaven with such majesty that even from a distance it strikes religious awe into the beholders . . . There are two vast towers that seem to salute the visitor from afar, and make the surrounding country far and wide resound with the wonderful booming of their brazen bells'. Henry VIII himself paid a visit to Becket's shrine with the Emperor Charles V in 1520 but by the time he expropriated the valuables from the tomb in 1538 there were few pilgrims.

Pilgrim badges

The medieval traveller collected souvenirs as does the modern tourist (pilgrims were requested not to chip pieces off shrines or carve their coats of arms on the fabric of the churches). The trinket or badge associated with a particular shrine was proof of the pilgrimage; it also identified the traveller as a pilgrim and therefore a person to be treated with charity. The badges were often supposed to have some of the miraculous power associated with the shrine.

The badges were cast in stone moulds and were usually of lead or poor quality pewter. Rich people sometimes had tokens in more expensive materials, but few of these have escaped the melting pot. At some shrines the badges were made in the priory – as at Walsingham – or in the town itself, as at Canterbury, where they were sold to pilgrims in shops just outside the cathedral gate.

Every pilgrimage had its special sign or badge: a palm for the

40. Mould for a pilgrim badge

Holy Land (hence the name Palmer), the cross keys of SS Peter and Paul or the vernicle for Rome, St Catherine's wheel for Sinai, the Virgin and Child for Walsingham; there was also the axe of St Olave, the horn of St Hubert, and the comb of St Blaise. Most common of all badges was the scallop of Compostela; St James of Compostela was the patron saint of all pilgrims. Canterbury had two main types of badge, the ampulla or miniature flask which held drops of the martyr's blood and was stitched onto clothing or hung around the neck; and the head of St Thomas wearing his mitre. Canterbury bells, inscribed 'campana Tome' were also made and effigies of the shrine with a large stud representing the Regale of France.

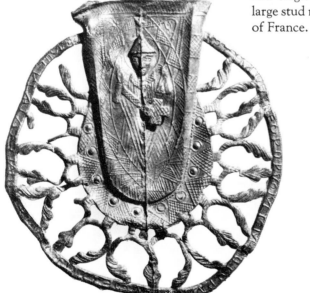

41. Pewter ampulla showing Becket

42. Mitred head of Becket

40

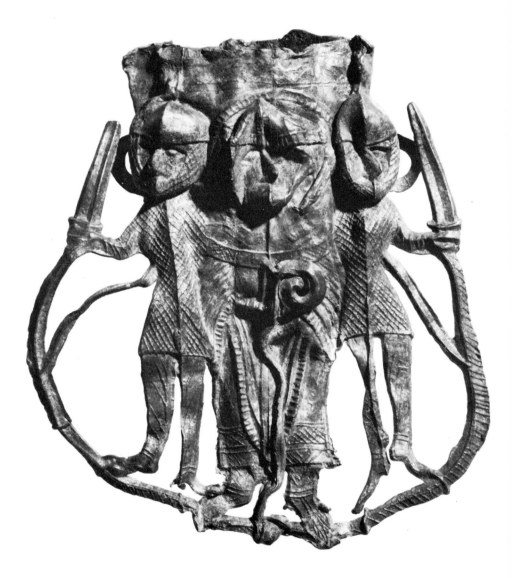

43. Ampulla showing Becket and his murderers

44. The Black Prince

8 the Black Prince

Edward Plantagenet, son of one king and father of another, was called the Black Prince probably because of the colour of the livery worn by his retainers. In his lifetime and after his death he was a hero of the English, a symbol of bravery in war, chivalry, and social splendour.

The Prince always had a special affection for Christ Church and was a visitor there from his childhood. He was born in June 1330, the son of Edward III and Queen Philippa; his younger brother was John of Gaunt. Edward had the fierce Plantagenet temper but he was a religious man. In 1345 he was knighted by his father although he had done little to earn the honour as was customary at the time; he did not win his spurs until the following year at the battle of Crécy. His mottos were 'Houmont' (courage) and 'Ich Dien' (I serve). He was one of the first members of the Order of the Garter, the great order of chivalry founded by his father.

The English victory at Poitiers in 1356 was in part due to Edward's skill and courage as a commander in battle. He took King John the Good of France prisoner but treated his captive with courtesy; the men visited Canterbury together and made offerings at the shrine of St Thomas.

In 1361 the Prince married Joan Plantagenet, the Fair Maid of Kent. She was his cousin and papal dispensation was required for the marriage.

In 1363 he endowed a chantry in the crypt of the cathedral which had two altars and was served by two priests. He also gave to Christ Church his manor of Fawkes Hall; this property, now called Vauxhall, was taken over by the Church Commissioners in the nineteenth century and became one of their most profitable holdings.

45. Shield

The Prince was made Duke of Aquitaine and Gascony the year after his marriage and he and his Princess lived in Bordeaux in great splendour. His son, Richard of Bordeaux, later Richard II, was born there in 1367. The magnificent court and the army maintained by the Black Prince cost a huge amount of money and the heavy taxation needed to finance these eroded his tremendous popularity. He further offended his subjects by appointing Englishmen instead of Frenchmen to senior posts in his duchy. Rebellion broke out against his rule. Nevertheless the Prince invaded the neighbouring territory

46. Gauntlets

and besieged Limoges. When the city fell, he had three thousand of the inhabitants, men, women and children, massacred.

When Edward returned to England in 1373 he was already a sick man and on 8th June 1376 he died. His cruelty was forgotten, extravagance was not considered to be a fault in those days, and he was remembered as the flowering of English manhood. In his will the Prince had asked to be buried in the chapel of Our Lady Undercroft, but he was such a national hero that it was thought more fitting to bury him in the Trinity Chapel near the shrine of Becket.

47. Jupon

48. The enthronement of Donald Coggan, 24th January, 1975

46

9 archbishops

Christianity first came to Britain during the Roman occupation; it gradually spread through the province and when the Roman legions were withdrawn many Christians remained. There was a Christian community in Roman Canterbury, or Durovernum as it was called, but by the middle of the fifth century the Anglo-Saxon invaders were in control of the whole of Kent. The invasions almost wiped out Christianity in England, it only survived in Wales and parts of the west country and in Ireland.

Augustine (597–c.604)

In 597 Pope Gregory the Great sent missionaries to convert the English. A monk called Augustine was chosen to head the mission; he set out with some trepidation and even tried to turn back. However, when he landed in Thanet he was well received by Ethelbert, the King of Kent and the most powerful ruler in England at that time. The King's wife, Bertha, was the daughter of a Frankish ruler and was already a practising Christian with her own chaplain and place of worship, St Martin's Church, which is still standing.

Ethelbert himself soon adopted Christianity and on Christmas Day 597 Augustine is said to have baptised over ten thousand converts in the Canterbury area. The monastery of St Peter and St Paul (later renamed St Augustine's) was founded just outside the city wall, the church that had been used by the Roman Christians was rebuilt, and another see was established at Rochester.

When he felt that his foothold in England was secure Augustine travelled to Arles to be consecrated Archbishop of the English. Later he received from the Pope a pallium (a cloth band that rests on the shoulders); although the pallium was not an official symbol of power

49. Augustine, from a 15th century
Lives of the Saints

50. English dioceses at the time of
Theodore of Tarsus

it became the badge of the archbishopric and still figures in the arms of the see of Canterbury.

In spite of the number of converts he made, Augustine's mission was not an unqualified success. He never managed to move his own base to London as he had intended. But his most serious failure was in his relations with the Celtic Christians.

The Celtic Christians had been cut off from Rome by the barbarian invasions and in isolation had developed their own customs and practices. Augustine dealt with these difficulties tactlessly and conflicts developed between the two churches which were not resolved until the Synod of Whitby in 664.

Theodore of Tarsus (668–93)

Superficially England was quickly Christianised, but there were many later lapses into paganism. It was not until Theodore of Tarsus came to the country that the whole of England acknowledged and obeyed the archbishop of Canterbury.

During the seventh and eighth centuries the church gradually changed its character from that of a missionary church to an established organisation. It consolidated its hold on the population and the parochial system gradually began to develop.

Theodore was already an old man when he came to Canterbury, but he was archbishop for twenty-one years. He was responsible for dividing the country into sees and establishing the organisation of the church at the councils of Hertford and Hatfield. He was also a wise and scholarly man and he founded a centre of learning at Canterbury that has been described as the first univeristy in the English-speaking world.

48

51. Dunstan at the feet of Christ

52. Alphege, from a roof boss in the cloister

Dunstan (959–88)

Dunstan was a remarkable man. He became a monk at Glastonbury and later was Abbot there. He reformed the monastery, insisting on strict observance of the Benedictine Rule. This led to a revival of monastic life in England which had almost disappeared after the Viking invasions; he founded or refounded the abbeys at Christ Church, Canterbury, Malmesbury, Westminster, Bath and Exeter among others. Dunstan was also a great statesman and acted as minister and treasurer to the kings of Wessex. After becoming archbishop he continued his reform of church life; he also first established the coronation rite of the English sovereign.

Dunstan was a man of learning and skill as well as a churchman and statesman. He was an accomplished musician, an illuminator of manuscripts, a metalworker and a bell-founder.

Alphege (1005–12)

In the year 1011 Canterbury fell into the hands of the Danish invaders. The Archbishop, Alphege (or Aelfheah), and his monks took refuge in their church. The Danes set fire to the building and many of the monks were killed by the molten roof lead falling on them. Alphege himself was taken prisoner and held to ransom, but he would not allow the people of Canterbury to pay the ransom. After months of imprisonment he was set upon and killed by a group of drunken Danes in Greenwich. His body was ransomed by the people of London and was buried in St Paul's, but in 1023 his remains were translated to Canterbury and enshrined in the presence of the Christian King Cnut who laid his crown over the high altar to expiate the murder done by his countrymen; he also gave large tracts of land at

49

53. Lanfranc, from a Norman
    manuscript, c.1100

54. The murder of Becket shown in a
    cloister roof boss

Sandwich to Christ Church. Though he had not died for the faith, Alphege was considered to be a martyr since he had died to save his tenants from further exploitation and extortion.

Lanfranc (1070–89)

Under the Saxon archbishops the primacy of Canterbury had become somewhat shadowy but Lanfranc, who has already been mentioned because he was responsible for the rebuilding of the cathedral after the fire of 1067 and for re-establishing the monastery, played a key role in the development of the archiepiscopal see of Canterbury. He was a Norman and a friend of William the Conqueror, but in spite of his power Thomas, the Archbishop of York, would not recognise the supremacy of Canterbury. The dispute was taken to Rome, but the Pope referred the matter to a council of bishops and abbots which met at Winchester in 1072 in the presence of the King. The Accord of Winchester established the primacy of the southern archbishopric.

Anselm (1093–1109)

After the death of Lanfranc the see was vacant for four years – William Rufus was in no hurry to appoint a successor as in the interim he received the revenues of the see. Like his predecessor, Anselm had been Abbot of Bec. He was often in conflict with the king, indeed he spent a great part of his primacy in exile. He was neither a clever politician nor a particularly effective statesman, but was a saintly man better suited to a cloistered life of scholarship. He was one of the most original thinkers of the early Middle Ages and wrote several philosophical and theological works which influenced the thought of his time and earned him the title of 'the father of Scholasticism'.

Thomas Becket (1162–70)

Thomas of Canterbury, Thomas à Becket, revered as a martyr by millions and as a saint by many, is perhaps the best-known figure associated with Canterbury. He was born in Cheapside and always referred to himself as Thomas of London.

Thomas had prosperous Norman parents and received a good education. He entered the household of Archbishop Theobald where his talents were recognised and he was recommended as a secretary to the young King Henry II. Thomas and Henry were both vigorous and able men, they became strong friends and led extravagant and worldly lives. The King made Becket his Chancellor and as politician and soldier Becket served the King loyally.

In 1162, at Henry's instigation, Becket was made Archbishop of Canterbury. Becket was no longer the king's man but became the church's man. He was ordained a priest after his appointment but he never became a monk (although he was the titular head of the monastery of Christ Church). He devoted himself to his new duties and led an ascetic life; after his death it was found that he wore a monk's hair shirt under his fine episcopal robes.

Conflict between the church and state had been simmering for some years. Between Becket and Henry the row blew up over the immunity of the clergy from the King's jurisdiction. Once more the Primate of All England went into exile. There was a reconciliation between the two men, but the seed of their final conflict had already been sown. The King was often abroad and he wanted to have his son crowned to ensure the succession. In the absence of Becket this ceremony was performed by the Archbishop of York. Becket was furious and on his return to England he got the Pope to suspend the Archbishop of York, but he did not tell the King what he had done. When Henry heard of Becket's activities he was enraged and uttered the famous words 'will no-one rid me of this low-born priest?'.

Four of the King's knights, Reginald Fitzurse, Hugh de Moreville, William de Tracy and Richard le Breton, immediately set out for England to fulfil the King's rash wish. The Archbishop knew that he was in danger but continued to perform his duties in the cathedral. The knights tried to get Becket outside the church, for the crime of sacrilege was much more horrible to the medieval mind than the crime of murder, but they were eventually forced to slay him in the transept which has since been known as the Martyrdom.

Almost immediately after Becket's murder miracles became associated with his tomb and there was a tremendous wave of emotion which spread all over Europe: Becket became a cult figure; he was canonised in 1174 and his tomb, first in the crypt and then in the Trinity Chapel, was a centre of pilgrimage until the Reformation.

Hubert Walter (1193–1205)

Archbishop Hubert Walter was more remarkable as a powerful and conscientious civil servant than as the spiritual leader of his country. By the end of the twelfth century affairs of state and the administration of government had become very complicated and needed to be run by educated men; and the church had a virtual monopoly of education. Richard I, who was King from 1189 to 1199, was only in England for a few months during his entire reign and in his absence Hubert Walter acted as Chief Justiciar. He accompanied the King on the Third Crusade, and on his return to England raised the ransom for the King's release from captivity. After the death of Richard the Archbishop was Chancellor under King John, whom he had crowned in Canterbury cathedral. One chronicle describes him as 'tall of stature, wary of counsel, subtle of wit but not eloquent of speech.' On hearing of his death, King John is quoted as saying 'now I am truly King of England'.

In 1890 the tomb of Hubert Walter was opened on the rather dubious pretext of identifying the remains within. In the coffin was the body of the Archbishop in full pontificals. Those vestments which were made of silk had survived and are superb examples of twelfth century weaving and embroidery.

Stephen Langton (1207–29)

Like Dunstan, Anselm and Becket, Stephen Langton spent part of his primacy in exile. He was appointed by the Pope, Innocent III, and King John was so enraged at not having had his own man in Canterbury that he would not let Langton into the country. When the King had submitted to the Pope, Langton was again out of favour for his support of the rule of law and order and increasing the power of the barons: this was the conflict that led to the Magna Carta crisis of 1215.

It was Stephen Langton who divided the Bible into chapters – almost into the form that we still use. He was also the first archbishop to live at Lambeth Palace which was conveniently near to the centre of power at Westminster.

Simon Sudbury (1375–81)

Simon Sudbury, who made generous contributions to the rebuilding of the nave of the cathedral, was another churchman who played a prominent role in affairs of state. He was an adherent of John of

55. Seal of Stephen Langton

56. The tomb of Henry Chichele

Gaunt and it was he who crowned the Black Prince's son, Richard II, in 1377. He was something of a king's man and worked for co-operation between church and state and towards the end of his primacy he became Chancellor. As such he was held by the people to be responsible for the hated poll tax. During the Peasants' Revolt the archbishop took refuge in the Tower of London, but he was captured by the rebels and beheaded.

Henry Chichele (1414–43)

No visitor to Canterbury can fail to be aware of Chichele because of the magnificence of his tomb. He was a skilled administrator and diplomat and a friend of Henry V, but his primacy was marked by difficulties with Pope Martin V which did much to undermine the authority of Chichele in England. He was educated at Winchester under the patronage of William of Wykeham and is remembered today as the founder of All Souls College, Oxford. Chichele, who was a good friend of Prior Chillenden, spent thousands of pounds on the cathedral; he is believed to have provided the money for the building of a new library, for the Oxford Steeple, and for the cloisters.

Thomas Cranmer (1533–66)

During the crucial period of English history when the church in this country officially broke with Rome, Thomas Cranmer was Arch-bishop of Canterbury. Immediately after his appointment he annulled the marriage of Henry VIII and Catherine of Aragon and three years later he did the same for the King's marriage with Anne Boleyn and then again for Anne of Cleeves. Although apparently subservient to

57. Thomas Cranmer, c.1548

58. Cardinal Pole, after Sebastiano del Piombo

the King, Cranmer was a sincerely religious man. He became more and more protestant in his views; he played a large part in the dissemination of the Bible in English and the destruction of images and relics in churches. Cranmer was a scholar and a theologian, not a politician, and he hoped to regain some of the simplicity of the early church. His greatest memorial is the Book of Common Prayer.

When Mary Tudor acceded to the throne the country was reconciled with Rome and Cranmer was tried first for treason and then for heresy. In a moment of weakness he recanted and accepted the authority of Rome; however he later reasserted his own beliefs and for them he was burnt at the stake in Oxford in March 1556.

Reginald Pole (1556–58)

When the church in England was reconciled to Rome during the reign of Mary I, Cardinal Pole was made Archbishop of Canterbury. He was of royal blood but he had opposed the divorce of Henry VIII and had gone to live in Rome. Pole restored the mass, refounded monasteries, and did everything he could to promote a counter-Reformation. A fierce persecution ensued, and hundreds of protestants were burnt at the stake.

The Queen was more unpopular with her subjects for her marriage to Philip of Spain – who thus became King of England – than for her religious beliefs. Her death in 1558 must have seemed providential. Cardinal Pole, the last Roman Catholic Archbishop of Canterbury, died a few hours after the Queen.

The Elizabethan Settlement of the following reign gradually established a church in England that was independent of both Rome and Geneva, and defined a new relationship between church and state.

59. Archbishop Laud, by Van Dyck

William Laud (1633–45)

Laud was a High Church man. He set himself against the Calvinistic beliefs of the time and attempted to enforce liturgical uniformity on the church – to the intense anger of the Puritans. He was a scholarly man; before becoming Archbishop he was Chancellor of the University of Oxford where he carried through much-needed reforms, and he played a leading role in affairs of state.

Laud was a passionate reformer, determined to impose his ideas on others. There was need for reform: many churches were in a state of physical and moral decay, but he lacked tact and pursued his reforms too ruthlessly. He went so far in his opposition to puritanism that the King was forced to suspend him from office and he was later impeached by the Long Parliament and imprisoned in the Tower. In January 1645 he was beheaded. After his death the see remained empty for fifteen years.

William Juxon (1660–63)

At the execution of Charles I in 1649 the Bishop of London, William Juxon, was in attendance. During his imprisonment the King and the Bishop became friends. On the last day of the King's life Juxon read the lesson of the day to him – it happened to be the story of the crucifixion.

Juxon had been a loyal follower of William Laud, but like the other bishops he coasted through the period of the Commonwealth. After the Restoration in 1660 and at the age of seventy-eight, he was elected Archbishop of Canterbury. He was a benefactor to the cathedral and he gave the wooden doors of Christ Church gate which bear his coat of arms.

60. Archbishop Howley breaks the news of her accession to Queen Victoria

61. Fresco given to Archbishop Ramsey by Pope Paul VI

During the eighteenth century the archbishops tended to be involved primarily in national and political affairs, and were half-hearted in the performance of their diocesan duties. The links with Canterbury were slight, even their enthronements were enacted by proxies.

William Howley (1828–48)

William Howley, who became Archbishop in 1828, was in many ways an eighteenth century High Church man. He was the last of the archbishops to wear a wig. He was an extreme Tory of the old school and opposed any political or educational reform as well as rights for Catholics and Jews. On the death of William IV it was Howley who went to the young Princess Victoria and announced her accession to the throne.

In the first half of the nineteenth century an archbishop was not so overburdened with work as he is in the 1970s; at Lambeth 'the general post letters in the morning for the Archbishop and Mrs Howley were put in a china bowl in the hall. They were scarcely enough to cover the bottom of it'.

At the time of the Reform Bill in 1832, the bishops, and Howley in particular, were very unpopular with the masses – who saw them as being opposed to any reform – and the Archbishop even applied for an armed guard at Lambeth. Although he did allow considerable reform within the Church of England, Howley himself was the last of the 'Prince-Archbishops'; he rode from Lambeth to Westminster in a coach with outriders whereas his successor, Sumner, walked the distance with an umbrella under his arm. After Howley's death the revenues of the archiepiscopal see were controlled by the Ecclesiastical Commissioners.

Archbishops in the twentieth century

Frederick Temple, who was archbishop at the turn of the century, rebuilt a residence in the precincts at Canterbury and this helped to restore the connection between the archbishop and his see. Randall Davidson who succeeded him guided the church with great skill and wisdom through the difficult years from 1903 to 1928 and he revived much of the prestige of the primacy.

One of the men who did most to democratise the church and make it better suited to its task in the changed conditions after the First World War was William Temple, the only man ever to follow his father at Canterbury. Temple is considered by many to have been the most brilliant archbishop since Anselm and his influence was felt in the fields of politics, philosophy and education. He was a convinced socialist and much loved by the people. His sudden death in 1944 was one of the most shattering blows sustained by the Church of England in recent times.

During this century the spread of the world-wide Communion of Anglican Churches has enhanced the importance of Canterbury since the Archbishop is recognised as the first Bishop of the whole Communion.

In 1960 the then Archbishop of Canterbury, Geoffrey Fisher, visited Pope John XXIII. This was the first time that the primate of England had met the head of the church of Rome since 1397. This contact between the churches and the whole ecumenical movement which was eagerly fostered by Michael Ramsay, is a most striking – and encouraging – development of the twentieth century.

glossary of architecture

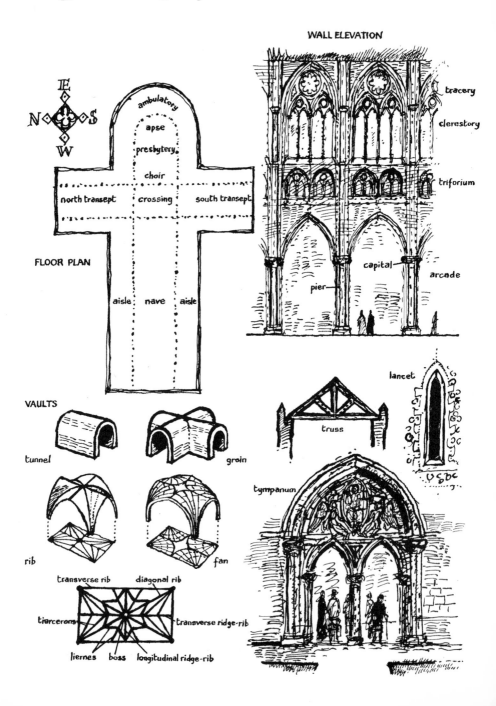

WALL ELEVATION

tracery

clerestory

triforium

capital

arcade

pier

FLOOR PLAN

E

N — S

W

ambulatory

apse

presbytery

choir

north transept   crossing   south transept

aisle   nave   aisle

VAULTS

tunnel

groin

rib

fan

lancet

truss

tympanum

transverse rib   diagonal rib

tiercerons   transverse ridge-rib

liernes   boss   longitudinal ridge-rib

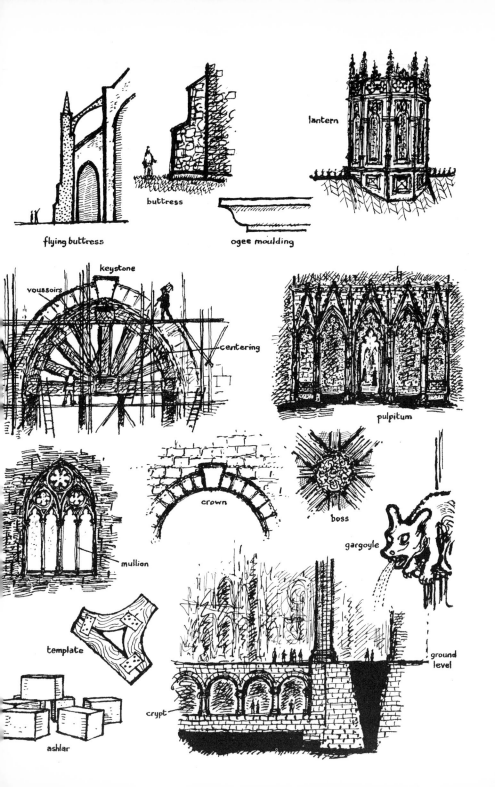

flying buttress

buttress

ogee moulding

lantern

keystone

voussoirs

centering

pulpitum

crown

boss

gargoyle

mullion

template

ashlar

crypt

ground level

glossary of vestments

dalmatic

pallium

amice

chasuble

alb

chimere

mitre

orphrey

apparel

crozier

maniple

cassock

scarf

cope

buskins

hood

surplice

tunicle

rochet

stole

fURtheR ReaDing

Memorials of Canterbury Cathedral,
E. Woodruff and W. Danks, Chapman & Hall, 1912.
Canterbury Under the Angevin Kings,
William Urry, Athlone Press, 1967.
Cathedral Architecture,
Hugh Braun, Faber, 1972.
The Cathedral Builders,
Jean Gimpel, translated by Carl F. Barnes, Grove Press Inc., 1961.
The Master Builders,
John Harvey, Thames & Hudson, 1971.
The Mediaeval Mason,
D. Knoop and G.P. Jones, Manchester University Press, 1933, 1967.
Discovering Stained Glass,
John Harris, Shire Publications, 1972.
Christian Monasticism,
David Knowles, McGraw Hill, 1969.
English Mediaeval Pilgrimage,
D.J. Hall, Routledge & Kegan Paul, 1966.
Pilgrimage, An Image of Medieval Religion,
Jonathan Sumption, Faber, 1975.
Cantuar, the Archbishops in their Office
Edward Carpenter, Cassell, 1971.
Thomas Becket,
David Knowles, A. & C. Black, 1970.
Saint Thomas Becket,
Herbert Waddams, Pitkin Pictorials, 1971.

Old texts which are available today:

A History of the English Church and People,
Bede, Penguin Books, 1968.
Of the Burning and Repair of the Church of Canterbury,
Gervase, edited by C. Cotton, Friends of Canterbury Cathedral, 1956.
On Divers Arts,
Theophilus, translated by Hawthorn and Smith,
University of Chicago Press, 1963.

For children:

Cathedral, the story of its construction,
David Macaulay, Collins, 1974.
A Visit to Canterbury Cathedral,
Althea, Cathedral Gifts Ltd, 1975.
The Murder of Thomas Becket,
Jackdaw/Jonathan Cape.
The Dissolution of the Monasteries,
Jackdaw/Jonathan Cape.

pictuRe cReOits

Royal Museum, Canterbury: 1, 27, 28, 29.
Cathedral Archives and Library/Derek Mossman: 3, 4, 19, 21, 23, 25, 31, 32, 33, 34, 35, 36, 55, 57.
Cathedral Archives and Library/Anne Oakley: 30.
S. W. Newbery: 6, 7, 8.
Mick Hales: 12, 13, 14.
Whitechapel Bell Foundry: 16, 17, 18.
Trinity College, Cambridge: 20, 22, 26.
R. H. Brasier: 24, 25.
Huntingdon Library, California: 37, 38, 39.
British Museum: 40, 41, 42, 43.
Department of the Environment: 45, 46, 47.
The Times: 48.
Lambeth Palace/Derek Mossman: 61.
Lambeth Palace/Courtauld Institute: 58, 59.
Bodleian Library, Oxford: 51, 53.
By gracious permission of H.M. the Queen: 60.